PET POEMS

(also not just pets)

Poems by Sean Petrie
Art by Amanda Hoxworth

BURLWOOD BOOKS
Austin, Texas
BurlwoodBooks.com

First published in the United States of America
by Burlwood Books 2021

Text copyright © 2021 by Sean Petrie
Art copyright © 2021 by Amanda Hoxworth
Cover design by Andrea Couch Wofford

ISBN 979-8-9850784-0-4

1. Pets—Poetry 2. Animals—Poetry 3. Human-animal relation-
ships—Poetry

*To my very first pet, Candy Cane, who was a
dachshund-Doberman mix. (Really.)*

- Sean

*To the pups that got me through the past few years, and
all the storytimes we'll share. Also Seth –
I love you and stuff.*

- Amanda

*To all the humans who've discovered it's too peopley out
there and you'd rather stay home and read this book to
your dogs while tucking them into bed.
Y'all are our spirit animals.*

- both of us

CONTENTS

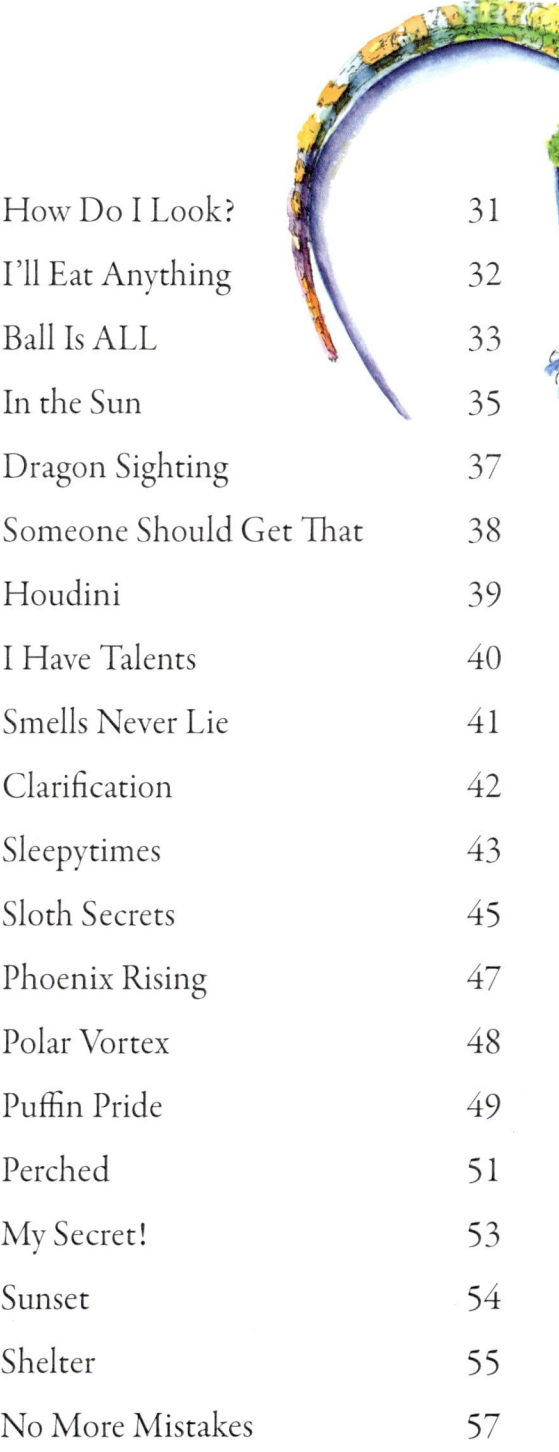

How We Got Here

Some things in life are planned and plotted out, like a bear building a den for hibernation. Others are a series of accidents and whimsy, like a dog playing in snow for the first time.

This book is a bit of both.

In 2017, Amanda suffered a traumatic car crash that nearly made her give up art. With severe brain and spine injuries, her creative spark seemed lost. But in 2019, she got a watercolor subscription box as a gift from her husband, tentatively tried it out … and found a new artistic footing, vastly different from anything she'd done before: the eclectic style of spatter and chaos you'll see on these pages.

In 2013, Sean had no inkling of being a poet. But when a friend asked him to join a one-day experiment—making up poems for people at a craft fair—something flickered. And then, crafting lines on a typewriter, based on each person's unique request, something ignited. Sean helped found Typewriter Rodeo, writing tens of thousands of poems for strangers all across the country.

Then, during the pandemic, the two of us met in an online art class (thanks, Becca Borrelli!), loved each other's style, and thought, "Hey, maybe we could do something together."

We started with "Bird Dreams"—inspired by Sean's poem, Amanda created the color-drenched bird you'll see later in these pages (and on the back cover). Then we flipped it—Sean looked at Amanda's paintings and tried to imagine what poems were hidden inside each animal, much like he'd done for thousands of people:

"What's going on with this dog?" ... "Why is this gecko so happy?" ... "If those jellyfish could talk..."

Like Amanda's spatterful style, Sean often wrote by instinct, flinging words and trusting where they would lead. And then suddenly, boom! We had a combination of art and poems that just, well, *worked*. Many were about pets. But others were about hippos and squirrels, lions and puffins and bears, oh my!

This book has a been a journey of accidents and exper-iments. Of delightful discoveries and inspiration. And the joining of two playful, passionate, and slightly quirky artistic styles.

We hope you enjoy it as much as a puppy in snow.

- Sean & Amanda

Workday

I understand.

I have eaten the food
All that you set out
I have lapped the water
Gotten the bowl to exactly
The halfway mark
I checked every window
Scared away two intruders
Dreamt of peanut butter
Sniffed each cushion for snacks
Twice.

Yes I understand
It takes a lot of time
To complete all the tasks
You are assigned.

Maybe now perhaps
You could take a tiny
Small break
From yours?

Dandelion

A weed
A pest
Is all some see

But I am soft
Like the breeze
I will flutter
Like your heart
And I will blossom
Into a million
Billion galaxies

All you have to do
Is pick
Me.

Party of One

I am alone
Happy and elated

A fly was here too
But I just ate it.

Foster

They say you can't teach
New tricks to old dogs

But I am new
To you
And I can learn any old trick
You want

I can learn to stay
Not to tug the leash
Too hard
(Except when we pass that one spot)
(And maybe that other one)

I can learn which things
Not to chew
(After perhaps a few tries)

I can learn which places
Are not the grass
I can learn which bed
Is mine

I can learn all sorts of things
That are old to you
Like how to call this
Home.

Fear

It comes in waves
Mostly at night
A creeping shadow
I see you, Fright

With eyes that blaze
And dripping fur
And all the rest
A formless blur

But I am quick!
I turn and flee
This time, Fear
You won't catch me

One day, though,
I'll stay and greet you
And with shaky gaze
I'll defeat you.

The Truth

We both know who
Broke the door screen
We both know who
Tracked mud on the carpet
It is our shared secret
Who ate the other half
Of the Pop Tart

And as everyone
Looks around
And wrinkles their noses
We both know where
That smell came from.

Smooshface

Just a moment ago
I jumped! I flied!
That's why my tongue
Hangs to my side.

I'm a little pooped
From playing around
So for now I'll rest
On this spot of ground.

But soon, oh yes!
I'll be ready, my friend!
To leap and smoosh
Your face again.

Responsibility

I did not ask for it
This mane that commands
Fear
This pride
I was born into
This strength and call and this
Hunger
I did not want it.
But we cannot choose
These things
Only choose
What to do
With the choices
We are given.

Family Dog

We know how it is
No calls on the phone
We know how it is
No one else at home

We know not everyone
Gets their perfect match
And we know that cold
Is not just what you catch

But we also know love
Isn't just for people!
Just like to be married
Doesn't need a steeple

Some are super lucky
With parents, partner, kids
But some have none of those
And maybe wish they did

But we know how it is
Just one person, that is fine!
You are warm enough for me
Just one person, I don't mind!

Every size is equal
Even one, just like this
Every size is love
We know how it is.

Beneath the Surface

In case of emergency
You can see by the bubbles
In case of emergency
You can bury your troubles

In case of embarrassment
You can sink in deep
In case of shame
You can just peep

In case of foul jokes
Or mean name-calling
In case it feels
Like the world is falling

In case of all that
Don't suffer those fools
Keep calm and collected
Keep low, and cool

Someday when you're ready
You will slowly arise
But for now you can show
All you need with your eyes.

Bunny Aid

I am here, my friend
To munch your sorrows

I will nibble
Those drooping worries
I will take them
In soft paws
Perhaps roll them around
Hop back and forth over them
(I am very good at that)
And who can resist
A good leaping?

Yes I am here, my friend
Just twitching
To help.

Are You Gonna Eat That?

I was wondering
Oh please-a please-a please-a
If I could have some (or just all?)
Of that leftover pizza

That hot dog perched
On the edge of your bun
You don't need it all
Maybe I could have some?

Also might I recommend
Not using a plate?
Or just let me clean it?
It's okay I will wait

And ohhhhhhhh me oh my
That filet mig-non??
Are you sure, are you certain
All of it's gone?

There's no need for garbage
Save the whole lot for me!
Oh except no thank you --
Not broc-ol-i.

Call Me Galaxy (Please)

I know, I know
It's not what you chose
That day at the shelter
When you saw me (yes!)
Curled in my shoebox
And "Lacey" jumped
Into your mind

It's a grand name
Graceful and clever
But I have also jumped
And grown a bit.

I do not mean to be
Disrespectful
I would never
(Except when I chewed your shoes)
(And scared the neighbor)
(And perhaps other times)

But who is perfect!
And we all grow
So why not names?

So call me Galaxy
(Please)
And please stay
Just as proud.

Up Dog!

Hey hey what is *up*?
Yup that's right the sky!
Haha that's my joke
I'm a really funny guy

Hey hey what's up *there*?
You fell for it again!
You looked at the sky
While I just licked your chin

Hey hey what is *up*!
Ok now it didn't work.
Now I kinda feel
Like a bad-joke-making jerk.

Now my tail won't wag
Now my ears just droop
Like I just dropped a big...
Delicious ice cream scoop!

Ha I bet you thought
I'd say something else!
That was my new joke --
I made it *up* myself!

The Dance

It's about the flowing
And gently glowing

Just ride the wave
Don't try and behave

No need to be smart
To perfect this art

Rise and fall, float and sway
There is no doubt, only play

Body parts don't need a name
Legs and arms, all the same

Flail and twist till you are numb
Don't overthink, just succumb

The dance is all, there's nothing more
Go out and glide – the world's your floor.

Medusa

Perhaps
You know the myth --
Those beguiling eyes
That mesmerizing hair.
Yes, every myth
Has a bit of truth
But I will only freeze you
For a moment.
Not forever.
Perhaps.

Stick

Why?
Because it is here.

You can toss it
Throw it with all your might
Cast it into the deepest weeds
Still
I will find it
Bring it back
Keep it close

Like you have done
With me
That day I was tossed
(I barely remember)
When I was left there
And you found me

I do not know
What "adopted" means
I only know
  Where I belong
    Where I stick
Where I will always
Keep coming back.

Ahhh Yes There

Oh I don't even --
I came over here for --
I can't remember
It doesn't matter

I just
Yes, yes please please please
Ohpleasescratchmethereyes

There is the spot
Behind myyyyy

Do you hear that thumping?
Oh sorry that was my leg

Yes the spot behind my ear
Yes yesssss
The left one, yes
And I was going --
Oh now the right one too?

I...

I...

I don't even remember
Where I am.

Friends?

I will step, yes?
But not too close.
I will lean, yes?
But just my nose.

Both our kind
Inspire fear
I promise not
To get too near.

You are wary...
So am I...
We both know how
Rumors fly.

They say the soul
Is in the eyes
Which one of us
Is in disguise?

Perhaps we are both
Misunderstood
Perhaps, one day,
Perhaps, we could.

How Do I Look?

Do you think I need another bath?
My nails?
Do they need trimmed?
I wasn't sure if perhaps this collar was appropriate?
There is the green one
I could wear that.

I have worked extra hard
Not to leave smells anywhere
(Though I don't understand that part.)
And of course I have made my eyes
Most alluring.

Yes, yes I think I am looking
Extra good.
I am ready for our walk --
Oh.

No that is fine
You go enjoy
Your other date.

I'll Eat Anything

Ah, I can smell them
Wafting from your humanness
All the swirling
　Bits of sadness

So come here!
Yes, right here
Scratch my ear
Or just let me lean
Against your leg

You can't see them
(You and your limited form)
But just relax --
I will breathe them in
　I will lick up
　　All your sorrows

It is okay
I have eaten worse.

Ball Is ALL

Why why why WHHHYY
Do you sip that drink
No time!
It is THERE RIGHT THERE AT YOUR FEET
Do you not see?
All you do is pick up
Ball
Right there, BALL
Pick up throw and I will be running leaping
CATCH
I will eat from the air
Twist and dance to SHOW YOU
Then drop the eaten air
THERE
It is RIGHT THERE
AT YOUR FEET
Just pick up throw again I will soar like

I have already forgotten

I will soar like I never have!
Why why why WHHHYY
Do you sip that drink
It is THERE RIGHT THERE
Do you not see?
Why would you ever want
To do anything else?

In the Sun

For all the ones
Whose faces
Have been on lamp-posts:
"If Found, Please Call..."
But no calls came.

For all the ones
Who bolted from the open door
Or dug beneath the fence
And never returned.

For all the ones
Who are still out there

I know it is hard
Oh believe me, I know

But I also know
There is sun
I also know
There is light
Everywhere and everyday

And I choose to see you there --
Wherever your there
May be
I choose to see you
Running happy
In the sun.

Dragon Sighting

There are lots of things
To be scared of:
Earthquakes
Snakes
The dark

But the scariest of all
Is the unknown.

Because have you ever seen a dragon?
Me neither.
Not yet...

Someone Should Get That

Um excuse me but
That food on the floor?
I think maybe now
That is mine not yours?

It looks so delicious
A new tasty meal!
I am sure you know
Exactly how I feel

And I am being good…
Patiently waiting…
It is very hard work
To sit here debating

It has now been forever
You still haven't seen it…
I think it's best for us all
If I quickly clean it.

Houdini

If I don't move
Don't flinch a feather
If I keep slanted
And still
Soon it will happen
Soon the sun
Will dip to just
The right spot
A star aligned
So that you
Will not be able to tell
Where I end
And light begins.

I Have Talents

I can wait.

This noise?
I can make it
For a long long very long time

I know your ears
Aren't the best
So it may take you a while
To notice

But I am very very good
  At watching
    And whining
      And patience.

Smells Never Lie

I hope I am not
Being too rude
I hope my proboscis
Doesn't protrude

You can say all the words
Scratch all the places
You can give all the treats
Make all the faces

But the truth is much more
Than meets the eye
Are you a good person?
Smells never lie.

Clarification

Um excuse me --
Pardon my stare
But are you going
To stay right there?

Or are you about
To dart and strike?
That is something
I do not like

I am just unsure
Of your intention
I'm rather cautious
Did I mention?

So if you could clarify
What you're about
And help to soothe
My waiting doubt

I would be the most
Grateful fawn
Friend or foe?
And let's move on.

Sleepytimes

My eyes are not drooping
Not even close!
I am just taking
A sleep-nappy doze...

With my eyes wide open!
And my tongue hanging low
And my fur part ocean
And part indigo

I am flying through clouds
I am swimming in seas
I am pooping out rainbows
And there are no fleas

The sun is my collar
The stars are my lashes
I solved string theory
And aced all my classes

I am DOG!
I am like no other!
And mmmmm yes the skyyyyy
Is all peanut butter.

Sloth Secrets

Well hello there, slothy
With your extra-long toe
Why oh why, slothy
Are you so   s   l   o   w?

I could send 5 txts
And take a drink
All in the time
It takes you to blink!

I could go to the store
Buy some shirts and pants
All in the time
It takes you to dance!

Wait—really?
Do sloths like to groove?
If you turn on the music
Will they get up and move?

Well now I know it
A secret no more!
They're just saving it up
Till they hit the dance floor.

Phoenix Rising

When I am done
When my anger is spent
My tantrum thrown
To the wind
When all that is left of my words
Is their wake
I will take a breath
And with the faint scent of ash
Let my kindness be
Reborn.

Polar Vortex

I get it
I mean, there you are
Way way waaaaaaaay up
In the bleakness
Where hardly anyone
Wants to visit
Yet you strut
Your snowy stuff
Like you are the land itself
Come to life!

No matter
If anyone ever sees.

Yup, I get it
Sometimes I spin
In quiet celebration
Of where I come from
Too.

Puffin Pride

No not at all
I ain't bluffin'
I ain't no turkey
Full of stuffin'

I'm a fancypants
Not ragamuffin
Head held high!
Afraid of nuffin'

On my noggin?
Not feathers fluffin'
I've got top-hat style
Every day I'm buffin'

Shining it clean
No time for scuffin'
This cap's my crown!
All you royals huffin'

And super jealous
But I'm not sluffin'
This hat stays put
Atop this puffin.

Perched

Please do not
Call me sheep
They are slow, shaggy
And always asleep

But I am sky!
I am sheer mountain-side!
I am climb-climb-climb-ing!
I am oh so alive!

I do not follow
Where I go I lead
I do not bleat
I have no need

No please never
Confuse me with sheep
There is no ending
There is only the leap!

My Secret!

Ahahahahaha
I have it here!
Yes yes yes
My precious dear!

I searched and scrambled
Branched and brambled
Leapt and climbed and even ambled
Until it felt like I was scrambled

But I am not!
Oh no no no!
I am quite sane
Assuredly so

I have caught it here
In my furry grasp
It is mine --
Mine at *LAST!!!*

Now if you please
If you wouldn't mind
I must go hide it
Where no one will find.

Sunset

There are advantages
To being different
I mean
I cannot gallop
As graceful as the gazelle
I cannot strike
As quickly as the lion
I cannot dash
As blur-fast as the cheetah
And perhaps I am not
As strong
As the elephant
Or water ox

Of course I hear
The hyenas laughing
Of course I know
The monkeys mock

But I do not mind
In fact I am proud
Of my awkwardness

For while they stay
In their low places
Or are confined
To their branches
I stand tall
Wherever I want
With the very best
View.

Shelter

I know what it's like
To hear strange noises
To be cold and afraid

I know
I remember

So don't worry
I will be here
I can hear
Evil
I can smell
Danger
I can see
Everything

I can keep you safe
I can rescue
Too.

No More Mistakes

This branch, my feathers
All of me shakes
I have made them all
All the mistakes!

I left the window open
I lost my shoe
I used waaaay too much
Super glue

I ate your brownie
I forgot to text
Who knows what
I'll mess up next!

That's why I've decided
To never ever fly
I can't make mistakes
If I never ever try.

Seeing

I see the snow

The way no one else
Takes the time to --
Each flake
A million choices combined
Into a shimmering
Twirling color
Like no other.

This is how
I see you.

Bird Dreams

I mean come on
If you could choose
Just one superpower
Nearly everyone would pick
Soaring, swift
   Flight

Where the air turns to streaming color
Where the stars are ripe for plucking
Where gravity is not a fight but a dance

And now you know
When an elephant raises its trunk
And trumpets its horn
It's usually because a bird
   Is flying over
And that's the elephant's way of saying
      "I wish."

The Ride

I feel
The wind
I bristle
With the touch
Of the breeze
I paw
  Gently
The giving earth
Still trembling
With the hoofprints
Of all who have run
Before

Then I see
The horizon
And go!
And it is a race
To see who can reach it first:
Me
Or the laughing wind
Along for the ride.

Still Got It

I don't know
What they're talking about.

I may be old
But right now I could roll over
Twice
If you wanted.

I could balance that tennis ball
On your shoe
While giving a high five
Then play the piano
If you showed me.

I don't know
What they're talking about
Right now
Ahhhh, right now
You could teach me...
  Right now I could do...
Anything.

Appreciate the Swallow

Oh forsooth thou friend
I shall tell a tale
Of my poor health
I was weak, frail!

I had the throat
Of strep, you see
And when I swallowed
It was pain -- times three!

Like needles and pins
Yon darning my throat
Like eating mush
Of glass, not oat

But that was a fortnight
Or more, ago --
Today I am healed
Huzzah! And lo!

Still forthwith I forsooth
To never forget --
And so each day
I stop, and let

My gullet gulp
Without pain, or wallow,
And simply give thanks
For the swallow.

(Did thou thinkest this poem
Was about the bird?
Hie hee no, my friend!
Don't thou be-est absurd!)

Traveler

How far have you gone?
How far have you come?

I have walked, padded, traipsed

Fields and forests
Mists and mountains
Lands and light years

All travelers
Wear a bit of their past
And future

Where have you been?
And where, oh where,
Will you go
Next?

Warmth

The way it feels
In your window spot?
When you turn your face
To the sun?

Or when you are curled up
In your latest find --
That safe-on-all-sides
Cardboard box
No one else wants?

Yup that's exactly me
With you at my side
(Are you purring
Or am I?)

So snuggle in
Let's close our eyes
And just be --
Because neither of us
Needs to see
A thing.

"Chicken"

Go ahead
Call me it again
Tell me how scared and clucky I am
Go ahead
Call me all the names
I know the true one.

Because inside
I am burning
And it is only a matter of time

I will fly from your taunts
From all the cages you can build
See them flutter
In flames.

And now
Shield your weak eyes

And now
Whisper my real name
  In awe.

After the Rain

Let's go explore
You said with your eyes

There is so much more
Your tail said

Than these stale walls
And the carpet we've walked forever

Out there is soft grass
Soft mud and softer puddles
Smells and hidden treats

Even a few of the flowers you like
(Though they do not taste
Like they look)

And so, while I love
The warm fire and cozy cushions
I will let you lead me
Across the cold and wet
Every time.

Bad Reputation

The word on the street
Is I like to fight
But does every rumor
Turn out right?

I just want to find
Where it is I fit
I am not a bull
My life not a pit

I'm full of soft licks!
Warm cuddles too!
I just want to be loved
(Maybe so do you?)

Haven't you ever
Been misunderstood?
We all deserve a chance
To turn bad to good.

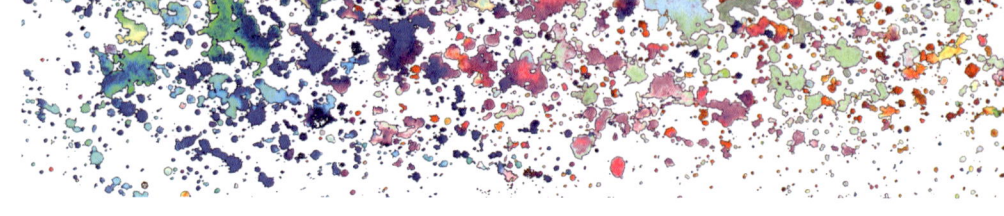

Why-No-Sir

I will tell you my story
Sad but true
I will tell it but once
And only to you

When I first arrived
There was joy in the world!
From the moment the tip
Of my horn unfurled

But then, a gasp
A squint, a silence --
"Where is its fur?"
Someone asked (in shyness)

They gathered around me
With manes of white
Elegant creatures
With horns so slight

But mine was a lump
Of putty and pudge
They were pure magic
I was pure sludge

"It is not one of us,"
They proclaimed (with grace)
And I knew that I
Was not in my place

So I departed forlorn
In search of my kin
I soon found the narwhals
But I could not swim

I found markhor and mouflon
But their horns were paired
I found Jackson's chameleon
But it ran away scared

I was called many names
None of them kind
But as my hide thickened
The less did I mind

Some waved from afar!
But as I got closer
The response was always:
"Oh. Why-no-sir."

I scoured desert and vale
Plied mountain and sea
Until at last I found
Another like me!

Its hide was pudgy
And so was its horn
This was no mouflon
And no unicorn

"You are my kind!
With snout so stout!"
But it did not move
Just spoke with doubt:

"I grew this horn,
To defend myself
Against the whole world
And a whole lot else."

I nodded with knowing
And a touch of shame
"I grew my rough skin
To do the same."

And so we moved closer
With each step more trust
And that's how we became
Why-no-sir us.

Winter Feast

Ah come with me now
Human, creature, beast
Come join me in
The winter feast

Where trees are salads
On upright bowls
Staying ever green
No matter how cold

Where the snowy ground
All around invites
Quench your thirst
Go on, take a bite!

Where the sky melts
The world is quiet
This is no time
To go on a diet!

Yes come with me now
Across this ridge
Where you never need
To close the fridge.

Old Ways

I am the storm
The coming wind
Feel the change
As I sweep in

Bring down the clouds
And all of space
It is time, Old Ways,
To be replaced

Your tired sun
Split to stars
What was only Yours
Is now ours

I am wisdom
Set alight!
I am fear and freedom
Taking flight.

THANK YOUS

Amanda

My Art Teachers: Sarah, for finding ways to make intimidating things feel not only approachable, but fun as well ... Rose, for seeing my creativity and style even when I couldn't and helping me find my artistic footing again ... and Becca, for teaching me to follow my intuition and (magically) find comfort in doodling again—you're basically a superhero—and of course for creating a safe space to create and connect with other artists (like Sean, for example).

Sean, for allowing me to borrow your words when I was unable to use my own.

My Treatment Team and Support System, for celebrating even the littlest wins with me, reminding me how far I've come, and wanting to write me a literal prescription for art when I was about to give up.

Seth, for navigating this entirely new world with me, sharing in my excitement, and playing the always-terrifying game of, *"Hey, what animal does this look like to you?"*

My Reference Photographers: Pixabay and Unsplash, for creating platforms that connect artists and allowing me to visually venture places I otherwise would not get to experience ... Maria, dog whisperer and photographer ... Shana, sloth watercolorist extraordinaire ... Austin Bulldog Rescue ... Michael, brilliant dog photographer ... and Brittanie, for your digitization genius, patience, and creativity.

My Models and Inspiration: Apollo, Artie, Baxter, Bear, Calypso, Cedric, Chance, Contagious, Copper, Drizzy, Evie, Fiona, Harvey, Izzy, Kitty, Maddie, Matsi, Midas, Packer, Simon, Tank, Teddy, Tucker, Violet, Wampa, and Zeke. It's a delight to see you on these pages.

Sean

The best proofreader (and mom): Linda Christman.

All the cheering and advice: Lita Judge, Jodi Egerton, Owen Egerton, Katie Sternberg, Cecily Sailer, Bethany Bengtson, Sandy Petrie, and John Petrie.

Believing in my poetry, and just being one of the most generous people on the planet: Naomi Shihab Nye.

The stellar cover design: Andrea Couch Wofford.

Leading the most magical and intuitive art classes ever (and introducing Amanda and I!): Becca Borrelli.

Every single person I've ever been fortunate enough to sit across a typewriter from, listen to your story, and write you a poem.

And of course the amazing, one-of-a-kind art that inspired all these poems, and just being an all-around awesome co-author: Amanda.

And from both of us, a huge thanks to everyone else not named here, human and non-human alike, who helped make this book a reality!

ABOUT THE AUTHORS

Amanda Hoxworth never dreamed she'd be doing this book.

Occasionally there are moments in life that divide it -- into the time before that moment ... and the time after.

Following a traumatic car accident, Amanda nearly gave up on her art altogether. Brain and spine injuries made so many things, including her creativity, feel completely foreign.

Two years later, it still hadn't clicked. She was ready to give up when her husband gave her a watercolor subscription box. It's not an exaggeration to say that it completely changed her life!

Amanda was totally bit by the watercolor bug. It's given her an incredible outlet during her recovery, and a totally new style.

She's barely shared this life-altering thing with the world. It felt delicate and fragile, like it too could disappear in a moment. After a ton of encouragement from friends and family, she's nervously-excited to share a small piece of her journey here. Find her at @spatterfulchaos (IG).

Sean Petrie started writing poems on a whim, when a friend asked him to make up poetry for strangers at an art fair.

Eight years later, he's written over 20,000 poems, mostly for strangers, and mostly on an old typewriter (like the 1928 Remington Portable No. 2 shown here!).

He and his friends also founded Typewriter Rodeo—a group of poets who travel the country crafting poems for people at various events, as well as recording weekly radio poems.

Sean's books include *Typewriter Rodeo: Real People, Real Stories, Custom Poems* (Andrews McMeel 2018), *Listen to the Trees: A Poetic Snapshot of West Seattle Then & Now* (Documentary Media 2020 – poetry silver medal, IPPY Awards), and the *Jett Ryder* adventure-history series for kids (JollyFish 2021).

Sean teaches poetry and writing for kids and adults, as well as legal writing at the University of Texas Law School. Find him at SeanPetrie.com.